TRIUMPH ON THE DOORSTEP
Some Say I Can

By L. Delia Girard

Copyright © 2014 L Delia Girard

I have tried to recreate events, locales and conversations from my memories of them. In order to maintain their anonymity in some instances I have changed the names of individuals and places, I may have changed some identifying characteristics and details such as physical properties, occupations and places of residence.

Dedicated to people who have had to rely on the support of others to live their daily lives. May you be blessed with triumph in your lives and with people who are passionate about helping you be all you were meant to be!

Contents

Preface 5
Chapter 1 – In the Beginning 9
Chapter 2 – Pace Setter 15
Chapter 3 – Set Free 19
Chapter 4 – Hope Arising 28
Chapter 5 – Uncaged 45
Chapter 6 – Words Unspoken 54
Chapter 7 – Back to the Past 58
Chapter 8 – A Team Triumphant 64
Epilogue 69

Preface

Some stories just need to be told. There are many that sit silent, quietly fading into the years, losing their power with age and forgetfulness. But they must be told. They must be resurrected. I've been blessed with amazing opportunities to be a part of many stories of triumph. Stories of people who are typically marginalized, forgotten, silenced or ignored. Join with me, celebrate these marvelous people, celebrate their victories and be inspired as I do my best to share their stories. My hope is that these stories inspire you to be a life changer.

Maybe we are somebody, or know somebody who stands on the doorstep, sheepishly waiting for life to unfold. We wait and we wait and year after year we miss the triumph behind the door because we didn't get the encouraging word, or the belief of someone important to us. Life's challenges, people's perceptions, our misconceptions of who we are continue to cripple us from taking that one step closer to the door knob, turning it, in trepidation, and with trembling foot stepping over the threshold into the triumphant place. We just needed an arm of guidance, a smile and show of support, someone to say "yes you can!" or "I believe in you" or "you are unique, beautiful and special" or "I value you". Over the years, I've consistently seen lives changed through such simple words and gestures.

What is it that holds us back from getting involved or from believing in others? Is it fear? What if I encourage someone in something and they fail? I will look bad, people won't trust me again. Is it fear of commitment? Sometimes we know it will take a lot of hard work if we encourage someone, it may mean more time and commitment than I'm willing to give. Many triumphs are years in the making, do I have that commitment?

Is it procrastination? I will get around to it. Next week rolls into next month, which rolls into next year and maybe the next decade? For me, my procrastination is so evident that I had ten years to write this book and I'm three years late. Believe me, I can relate. Whatever the reason for us holding back, we need to take the bull by the horns and make it submit to our desire to experience triumph, be it personally or for the benefit of another!

Once we step over the edge of fear and carve the time out of busy schedules or lists of excuses, we will experience the great blessing of triumph. We will open the door and share in the triumphs of others. Seriously! We were made to celebrate! We were designed to be victors! Take hold of it, embrace the possibility, set your mind on it and decide today to be different!

> Teeter totter, here I go,
> Up and down on what I know.
> Frightened of unchartered ground,
> What lies beyond? Is it sound?
>
> Should I step into the great beyond?
> Will there be shouts or a gentle song?
> I know not of the risk I'll take.
> All I see is what's at stake.
>
> But this is right to celebrate.
> Taking risks that seem far too great,
> May once and for all set one free.
> Triumph approaches steadily.

As I mentioned above, this book has been 13 years in the making, but there is one person who over the last several years has continuously encouraged me in my writing. My husband Charles consistently praises my written words, the blog, the poetry and the book. While I have procrastinated, he has encouraged me, for which I am truly thankful.

If it weren't for the beautiful people whom I have known and supported over the past more than a decade, there truly wouldn't be a book. Thank you to all of you who have inspired me to be a better person, who have opened your lives, who have been vulnerable and have trusted my judgement and my help. Though I've changed your names to protect your identities, I hope one day you will know what an inspiration you've been and how you have deeply impacted my life and the lives of so many around you, you are unsung heroes, this is my gift to you, I will sing your songs.

    I want to thank the amazing mentors and teachers I have had throughout the years. There have been so many who have mentored me into a firm foundation in my career and in my spiritual walk, I hope you all know who you are, I hope I never failed to express my gratitude to you. Without you it is likely I wouldn't care enough to pen this book. Your wisdom and grace has trickled down and no doubt affected the life of each person celebrated in this book.

    Mostly, I thank my God. It is He who has transformed my life, it is He who has taught me to love deeply and it is He who took mercy and rescued me out of my own adversity. It is He who has given me victory and made me triumphant. May He receive the glory for any positive ways in which I have helped or supported others. Any wisdom I have had has been from Him and from His word. I know that I would not be the person I am day without His guidance and example.

Chapter 1 – In the Beginning

The framework simply must be shared, I didn't go into the field of developmental services by accident, in fact, this career direction was well thought of, researched and best of all, God appointed.

When my youngest child went to school full time I decided I didn't want to go back to work in the field I was originally trained in, which was as a legal secretary. I'd recently become a Christian and because of the things I was learning about the tenets of the faith, I really sensed a need to be helping people in some way. I had no idea where to begin but happened to come along a course facilitated by Human Resource Development Canada. The course was six weeks long and explored 'what I wanted to do when I grew up', which was quite funny considering I was twenty nine.

After working through the personality, interest and aptitude tests, several weeks later, I was left with three top career paths that would work for me: X-ray Technician, Occupational Therapist or Special Education Teacher. At the time we lived in a small town in rural Ontario. A town that had only one community college and I realized that I couldn't train for any of these careers locally.

Since I was prepared to travel or do correspondence all I needed to really was to choose which profession I wanted to embark upon. Nothing really popped out at me, so as I often did in those areas in which I had no idea what to do, I began to pray.

The property behind the house slightly inclined, sloping into tall oaks and tangled vines. My feet crunched as I trod the upper area, snapping twigs and separating the little acorn's hats from the nuts. I loved those little acorns, there were none like that in Western Canada where I grew up. Picking one up and gingerly tossing it aside, I contemplated my life's direction.

"Lord, I have no idea, what I should do. What direction should I go?" Round and round I went, lap after lap of the property, and I was hearing nothing. "How long Lord, how many laps should I walk before I understand what I should do?" I sensed the frustration rising, then I realized I just needed to trust and wait.

My feet continued to tread on the long dry grass beneath my feet. Again, "Lord, please show me what I should do, I don't want to go in a direction that isn't right for me, surely you know me better than I know myself." Almost instantly a little boy came to my mind, his name was Christian, and he rode the school bus with my children, he had some special needs and was an absolute delight to anyone he came into contact with. I knew beyond a shadow of doubt what I needed to do, after seeing his little face, framed by the yellow school bus window, I just knew, the Lord had given me a clear answer.

I'd seen it before, the Lord giving perfect answers to prayer, how wonderful. He also brought to mind a scripture verse "Truly I tell you, whatever you did for one of the least of these brothers and sisters of mine, you did for me". The world may say "the least of these" but truly they are the first in the eyes of God.

Joy spilled out of me, I had an answer and a direction! Immediately I went to work researching, I needed a bachelor degree and education degree, then some specialty courses, I could do these things by correspondence. I went on as if pulled along by wild horses. I sent applications out to several universities and surprisingly I missed every deadline for the fall semester!

Once again, frustration overcame me and I whined to God, "but I thought You said to do this!! Why won't you open the doors? I don't understand!"

Eventually, months later, I had a spiritual temper tantrum, stomping my feet in rebellion. Although, several times the Lord had shown me exactly what to do, and I brushed it off as if I knew better.

The first time, I was at the local community college with the HRDC career discovery program. We were taken to the Developmental Services Worker program area. They didn't take us to every program area, but they took us to this one. I remember the red brick hallways and the echo of our facilitator's voice, but I wasn't really attuned how God was directing me.

The second time was when I was telling a friend about what I felt God was showing me to do, and she said "Gee Delia, have you heard of the DSW program at the local college?"

"Yes", I replied, "but that's not good enough, I need a bachelor degree."

After a while, I was totally exhausted and unemployed with no direction. I proceeded to stomp my feet emotionally and booked an appointment with the local job counselor.

Defeated, I entered her office as she patiently waited for me to spill my story to her. At the end of my long-winded spiel, I told her that all I wanted was a job since I missed all the university deadlines.

"Who in the area is hiring?" I inquired.

Quietly she said, "Well, Sears is hiring, that might be suitable for you, but based on the story you just told me, why don't you look into the DSW program at the local college?"

Sigh... I just shook my head. Inside I was chastising myself. "Lord, I can't believe I didn't listen the first time, I just know this is from you."

My reply was full of uncertainty. "It's August, there's no way I will get into the fall semester at this late date."

"Why don't you just try? It can't hurt to try can it?" She simply smiled as if nothing profound had happened that day. The next day I called the college and two weeks later was sitting in my first DSW class.

Here I was, back in college after ten years of being away from the classroom. After two weeks of Psychology, Current Issues, Applied Health Sciences, Behaviour Management and Social Issues I was insanely overwhelmed! I felt like I couldn't get a grip on the school and awesome mom balancing act. I sat in class and felt like nothing was sinking in. I wondered how on earth I would make it through the next two years. So I made an appointment with the Dean of the program.

Feeling foolish, I slunk into his office, sat down and stared at my feet. "I feel ridiculous, I'm in class and feel like nothing is sinking in. I feel like I'm going to fail. I'm not sure how I can do this for the next two years. Should I keep going?"

Fingers thoughtfully placed on his lips as if in deep contemplation, he quietly reassured me, "Delia, what happens when you are outside in the sunshine and you go inside, into a dark room with no lights, can you see anything?"

"No." I replied, "I suppose I wouldn't."

He continued, "But then what happens? Do your eyes adjust?"

"Yes, I guess they do eventually."

"Maybe after a few minutes you can make out shapes and then after a while recognize objects as your eyes adjust. Then it doesn't seem so scary does it?"

"No, that makes sense I guess."

"How long has it been since you've been in school?"

"About ten years."

"Think of it, it is like you are in that dark unfamiliar room, at first you can't see anything and it's scary, but eventually your eyes will adjust. You will begin to be more comfortable recognizing things. That's what will happen with you. You will adjust, just stick with it."

Of all the analogies, this made perfect sense. He was right, eventually I did adjust. By the grace of God my transcripts showed every course and practicum was rewarded with an A+.

Truly miraculous for a sheepish young woman who had little confidence and little belief in her own abilities. On top of that, and by the grace of God, I was awarded three awards over the two year period. One being the Governor General's Medal for Academic Excellence at the college level.

I can't tell you how this helped me understand that anyone can do anything with hard work and determination and by God's grace. I know it is this very achievement that helped me resolve to work hard for the people I would support in years to come. As I had triumphed, I believed anyone could, disability or not.

Chapter 2 – Pace Setter

Dale has to be the one man who set the pace for me in the beginning. As a special guest speaker, he came to our college to tell us about his experiences as a young person institutionalized in a hospital-like setting in Ontario. This was prior to the community living movement and de-institutionalization movement.

Being my first time exposed to someone with an intellectual disability, I had a little fear inside of me. What if I don't know how to act? What if I don't respond properly? What if I stare too much? What if, what if, what if. I'm sure that many people feel that way, when we see someone with a disability in public, we don't know whether to give eye contact. Would that be staring? We don't know whether to smile, would that be patronizing? We don't know whether to avoid them, would that be ignorant? I'm sure I'm not the only one who struggled with these crazy thoughts at some time or another.

When Dale was escorted by our professor into our lecture room, I felt relief. Dale was a tall man with a kind but serious demeanor. Funny enough, I could probably say the same about myself. He was somewhat awkward and fearful at first.

Looking back I realize that I can relate. The first time I had to present to my class in college, the assignment was to research a particular disability, learn everything possible about it, and then give a 15 minute presentation to the class. Let's just say that the presentation was more about preventative first aid. My class mates began begging me to sit down about five minutes into the presentation. My heart rate skyrocketed, the blood drained from my face and my breathing became close to hyperventilation. Dale's minor nervousness was toastmaster elite compared to my feeble attempt to share information.

Not too far into his presentation, Dale had an air of confidence. He had confidence in his story, he had confidence in his right to tell it, and he had confidence that his purpose in life was to share his story. He believed that he could educate college students about the history of people who were institutionalized and passionately persuade them to believe that all people have rights, dreams and possibility.

Dale talked about the mistreatment in the institution. Not to say that all people who were institutionalized were mistreated. Likely they weren't. However some, like Dale, were. Dale reported stories of abuse, physical and emotional, confinement, withholding of basic needs and a capping of his basic rights to choose activities and participate in daily routines and life giving purposes.

None of us were ready for the harsh reality of what Dale and others had gone through, for close to an hour we were on the edge of our seats getting a wake-up call to a cruel reality. We heard stories about the forced sterilization of people, and how people would line up to have their toothbrushes sprinkled with baking soda, then line up at the sink, brush, spit, wash face and on to the medication line, where people would receive their daily, docile inducing medications, God forbid should they be acting out and need to be controlled for bad behaviour. It reminded me of a farm operation, feeding cattle. I was horrified, sad and determined that I would never stand for any such treatment of any person under my care.

As time went by I learned more about the history of the institutionalization and that Alberta was a model for the eugenics movement, which was spurred on by the depression and financial hardships. Alberta established eugenics legislation in 1928 and was the first of the British Empire to do so, and may have been the focus of the Nazis in the 30's, due to this early legislation. Not many Canadians are aware of that, but they should be. We can learn a lot from our history, a simple Google search brings plenty of information on the subject.

I'm not sure if it was these stories or an innate, experiential burning desire for justice, but something began to come alive in me. I felt a rising up, a need to set myself on a mission to help people believe in their worth and possibility and advocate against social injustice with fiery fervency.

Thus, the stories unfolded, close to 15 years of stories, unfolding like daffodils on a warm spring day. I have life, I have purpose, I've learned so much, because the people in my life, those with disabilities have proven to be the most determined, loving and inspiring people I can ever hope to know. Thanks to Dale, the pace setter, I sensed a deeper set of values being formed, a flint-like core of justice emerging, the 'me' I knew, was changing and the change was good.

>Pace setters with foreheads like flint.
>
>Purpose lies before them.
>
>Dormancy never overcomes their spirits,
>
>As they strive to keep alive their passions.
>
>World changers, one at a time, as stories come unfurled.
>
>Humbly, they know not the impact they have made.

Chapter 3 – Set Free

It was a cold one, so cold that my nose hairs stuck together with each breath. I zipped up my coat higher 'til the zipper touched my nose. I was glad for the relief I felt on the lower part of my face.

Clumsily I dug in my pocket with a heavy gloved hand. Finally, I had separated my keys from the stash of doggy poop bags. Mental note, I must remember to put my keys in my other pocket, or get a doggy bag dispenser on the leash. Somehow I knew I would continue struggling, because that mental note was a long standing one that, even though irritating, would never resolve, it just wasn't important enough.

Quickly, I unlocked the door, flicked the lights on and began preparing for another day of activity at the day program. I loved my job, I couldn't believe I worked here, I loved the agency I worked for and the other staff members, and my boss and especially the people I supported. It might not be special education, but working with adults with disabilities was exactly where God wanted me. He had opened so many doors to get here, and the favour I was shown was truly amazing.

One by one, people started to trickle in, I was in the office reading notes and getting ready, they were out there, discussing the weekend. The other staff greeted people and helped to get coats on the right hooks. People were busy getting activities out, the coffee pot gurgled and fresh coffee aroma filled the air. There was one way to describe the atmosphere; comfortable. We were comfortable with one another, there was a lot of trust and we had a lot of fun.

After I had finished my office duties I came out and sat down with everyone after pouring a hot java with cream only. This was my kind of work!

Suddenly, along came Mary. She was a lovely middle aged lady, with white hair, and sky blue eyes. Everyone lit up when she arrived, she was well-loved by all. We greeted each other with a smile and she made her way to the back of the room to put her stuff away. Although, I noticed she didn't have much to put away, she was wearing only a fleece coat, which I would wear in the fall, and no hat, no gloves, no scarf, nothing to protect her from the harsh winter that I had just experienced on my way in. I wondered if anyone noticed the troubled look on my face.

Mary proceeded to make herself a coffee and then set herself up at the table with the rest of us. She unfolded her binder of paper and then her Bible and proceeded to copy the pages word for word.

"How are you today Mary?" someone asked. "Did you have a good weekend?"

Mary's blue eyes came alive with the engagement. But as she pondered her answer, her eyes became downcast. Mary has a disability which causes her to speak with an impediment, she struggled with articulating and we had to listen very carefully. She was exquisite at supplementing her words with actions, and at this point we all understood what Mary was telling us about her weekend. Quickly, I invited Mary to the office where she could tell her story in confidence, while I documented.

Today's documentation was added to a long list of allegations that Mary had made against the family member she lived with. From verbal abuse, to locking her in her room, to neglecting to provide for her needs, as I had seen by how she was dressed for winter, to withholding meals as punishment, hair pulling, hitting, you name it, she reported it. Report after report we were instructed to ask Mary if she wanted to live somewhere else. Each time she said no. We rephrased, reiterated, repeated and over and over again she said "No."

When I first started working at this site and began reporting to my supervisor I was given a background. We had to be careful, we had to watch our step with this family member. When the family member was approached about these things over a year ago, she became enraged, to the point of verbal and physical abuse of staff and then yanked Mary from the day program for more than six months. At least she was safe for six hours a day with us. But if for whatever reason Mary stated that she wanted to leave her current living situation, we would do everything in our power to make it happen for her.

The months passed by and on occasion so did the stories, but we continued on as usual. We ended up finding a job for Mary at the local thrift store. Our hope was that she could take some clothes home in payment for her services. She ended up taking home sweaters, coats, gloves and accessories such as a purse and a belt. We felt pretty happy that we helped her get the upper hand in her wardrobe appropriateness, and honestly, I can't remember whether we got flack for that from family or not. None-the-less, Mary was thrilled at the lovely items she added to her wardrobe, the friends she worked with and confidence she had developed in her work. It showed in the glow in her face.

It wasn't long before Mary came in one morning with tears in her eyes. I knew it was time for a closed door office meeting. Once inside she produced something that made me feel a deeper level of sadness for her. She showed me a sticky label that said "Lier" on it (yes it was spelled like that). Mary motioned and showed me how her family member had stuck it on her forehead, evidence of that showed in the white hairs that had been ripped out when the label had been removed. My heart sank, she understood what the label meant, and I could only imagine what kind of verbal attack accompanied the label application. She was visibly upset, like she had been completely humiliated and she'd had enough. Who knows who witnessed it, we can only speculate the events that caused her so much anguish by the twisted look on her face.

s I always had, I asked her if she wanted to leave home or if she wanted to go home at the end of the day. She so clearly said she wanted to leave, I scarce believed my ears, so I asked again, rephrasing this time. Again, she clearly said, "Leave". I explained that it would mean she would live with someone else and that we weren't sure who. She nodded.

Considering what she had been through, almost insurmountable obstacles, she had so much courage and resolve. We ended up contacting adult advocacy and a worker made it just in time before the family member arrived. We were so afraid, because we knew there would be a rash of fall-out and misunderstanding, not only with the family but also in the community.

We were right, the family member lost her mind, we tried to explain the allegations and that Mary had said she wanted to live somewhere else, and as an adult she had the right to make that decision. Emotions were high, she screamed and hollered, saliva sprayed, crimson face, and veins bulged. This was the beginning of fear for me.

My children went to school just across the road from where the family member lived. I feared being seen, I feared that she would lash out. I questioned if I had done the right thing. I knew that the police were involved and that I would be questioned. I feared being questioned. What would I say?

It finally happened, two constables from the local RCMP detachment showed up at the day program. I invited them into my office, they towered over me with every weapon imaginable hanging off belts and harnesses. The questions came, what was reported, what happened then, what happened before, after? I was so overwhelmed. However, I was completely appalled when one of the officers said, "Well, isn't that the way you punish these people?"

I don't think I have to explain what is wrong with that statement. She is fifty years old I thought. Would you punish your mother? Would you punish your aunt? I couldn't believe my ears, but I thought to myself, what a poor example we have set, we haven't taught the community anything about people with disabilities and how they should be treated, or what their rights are, and they should be treated with dignity and respect.

I felt the indignation rise in me and I became somehow more aware of the way I needed to combat the fear and become stronger for those whom I supported. If the police couldn't protect the people I support, then who would?

Within a few weeks Mary had settled into her new home in a neighbouring community. I got the chance to see her when I was there for a meeting. She looked absolutely amazing, she was wearing some beautiful new clothes, a little rouge and some lipstick and had the light scent of perfume on her. When she saw me she ran toward me with arms wide open and gave me the strongest hug that I think had ever had to that point. I wish I could say that this was her day of triumph, but sadly it wasn't, it wasn't long before the unspeakable happened.

A phone call came in from my supervisor, she calmly explained what had happened earlier that morning. It took me all my effort to hold back the tears and restrain my anger at the same time. While Mary was walking toward the day program after being dropped off by her caregiver, her family member and the neighbour flanked Mary, grabbed her by the arms on either side and pushed her into their van. The police were called, but did nothing, they investigated and believed that

Mary should be with the family member. They didn't really give an ounce of weight to our reports.

I really have no idea what the family member was saying in the community or to the police. I do know that I had people from a local church approach me, saying that they couldn't believe I would have Mary taken away from family. I also had other people say, "It's about time! I saw her dragged out of Walmart by her hair one time". I couldn't help but wonder why this person didn't report such abuse.

Our agency administration pushed and pushed for one last meeting with the RCMP to let Mary have one last say about what happened and where she wanted to live. Finally a date was set. At the last minute my supervisor called and said that she couldn't go with her. I called our administration office, as I felt this was far outside of my experience and scope. Again, that came up void, no one there could take her. It boiled down to me, only a year into my career and I'm faced with this? I was at my wits end.

The next morning, I gathered up my courage, the family member was to take Mary to the station, and I was to be there in case the police couldn't understand her. I was told that the interview was going to be taped and that this was the last time they would meet about this. The family member waited outside in their car.

When I saw Mary she threw her arms around me. I quietly explained to her what was about to happen.

"Mary, the police are giving you one last chance to tell them about what your family member did."

Mary looked a little confused, but then with squinted eyes nodded her head.

"Mary, trust God, He will help you." She nodded again.

"Just tell the police lady what you told me. Tell her about some of the things she did to you, just the way you told me okay?" Again a nod.

"She will ask you if you want to live with your family member, tell her what you want, she will listen okay?" Mary once again showed that she understood.

"And Mary, if you need my help, to help them understand what you say, I will help you okay?" Mary smiled, the tears in her eyes glistened.

The rest of the time you could have heard a pin drop, just the ticking of the clock. We waited for the constable in silence, but somehow peace was in the room. Finally, the constable arrived.

"Mary, there is a camera up there, we are taping everything you say. Can you tell me what your family member did?"

Without hesitation Mary, reiterated the label incident, she told of many things with clear diction and a sound mind, she was so mad about it she slammed the palm of her hand on the table. We both stood in amazement, I'd never seen that type of emotion or heard such clear diction out of her. My heart simply rejoiced!

"Mary, thank you for telling us these things, do you want to go home with your family member now?" questioned the Constable.

"No." Mary squinted through her tears.

"You can take her, we will make sure that the family member has no access."

As I drove Mary to the neighbouring community, I was in constant awe of how God rescues His children. I really believe He enabled her with clear diction and gave her the courage to tell the truth. In it, the door to triumph was flung wide and my dear friend Mary walked through it in confidence to her beautiful destiny.

> Little bird with broken wing,
>
> You've been set free, and healed, to sing.
>
> To soar the heights and sing in trees,
>
> To find your nest and live in peace.

Chapter 4 – Hope Arising

The two of us were positively trembling inside, slinking down in that over-sized pleather couch. Surrounded by all-knowing, best interest-minded, everyone-has-an-opinion professionals. Don't get me wrong, I strongly believe in professional consultation and advice, but this wasn't their annual support plan, it was hers, and she sat there quietly and sheepishly.

Sadly, she sat their voiceless. She had learned over the years to just listen and obey, or better yet, answer questions how you think they want you to answer them. Then every now and then lash out, throw things, swear, hit, because seriously, that's what gets a result.

My emotions were all over the board and my thoughts constantly needed to be checked. I'm a woman who has to work things through a milieu of cogs and wheels in my brain before thoughts can be voiced, and as a new supervisor, I didn't really feel like my voice had any real clout or validity behind it. Consequently, there we were, the two us, bonding with nothing but the couch, voiceless and frustrated.

After about an hour and a half of note taking, it was finally over and everyone had decided what was best for Debby, and with each 'goal', she nodded in reluctant approval. I went away with my notes and the professionals filtered out one by one with their notes, 'til next year that is. Some would see Debby on a regular basis, some maybe quarterly and the others not until next year. That is, unless a crisis arose.

"So Debby," feeling the need to debrief, "What are your goals?"

The look of inquisitiveness on her face indicated that she had never really thought about it. I wonder if she thought "I go to day program, I come home, and I'm told I need to have a bath twice a week, and take better care of my teeth, and cut down on my pop. Don't be silly, I have enough goals!"

"I mean, if you could do anything, anything at all, what would you do?"

"Really?"

"Yes, even if it seems impossible right now, what would your goal be?"

"To move out of this stinkin' group home, I hate it."

Struggling to not choke on my saliva with my deep breath of surprise, I managed to gurgle something out that sounds something like, "Wha? What do you mean, why?"

"I hate living here, all I do is get bossed around, I want my own place."

Talk about opening Pandora's Box! This was a first for me. How do I deal with this? I asked a straight forward question and got a blatantly honest answer in return. Why should I expect anything less? Why would she say this now? Why would she trust me with this? Once again, the wheels and cogs were working overtime, I was thinking danger pay should be in order.

Danger, to think the unthinkable, to dream an impossible dream, if I don't brush this notion off, what will I be in for as leader of this team? But if I do brush it off, then Debby's triumph may remain on the doorstep, waiting for help, waiting for someone who believes in her to assist her to turn the doorknob in trepidation, and take that first shaky, nerve wracking step over the threshold of the unknown. What if triumph was waiting on the other side?

As all these thoughts sifted and filtered in mere moments, I remembered what I had learned from the first agency I worked for, an agency accredited with distinction, and recipients of the Donner award for more than a decade now, people should absolutely direct their own lives, and we should do everything in our power to help them achieve whatever goals, whatever ambitions, whatever their choices are and however they would define them. And this truly was an echoing sentiment that I learned so prevalently in my college days.

"Debby, it's not going to happen overnight, you know that right? It's going to take a lot of dedication and hard work on your part. But as long as you are willing to work hard and learn the skills you need to be safe and happy in your own place, then you have my commitment as supervisor of this home to support you to get there."

"Really?" it's almost as if Debby was suspended in a cloud, like it wasn't possible, like she was trying to process the resurrection of a dream she had dreamed and let die. "How?"

"Well, we'll go at your pace, but you will have to learn a lot of things, from banking, to shopping, to staying safe in the community, and other stuff that we might not know is important now, things might come up later. Are you sure you want this to be your goal?"

Debby nodded and said nothing.

Two weeks at this place, and I've already set myself up for a challenge that I'm not sure I know how to face. What on earth was I thinking? What would my boss think? What would the staff team think? Oh Lord help me!

"You can do all things through Christ who strengthens you." Came to my mind again. This wasn't the first time this had come to mind, it should be a life verse I think. It came to mind when trying to get through college, it came to mind when dealing with the dark days of listening to Mary's stories and feeling powerless to help, and now here again, it was if the Lord spoke to my heart, I may not know what to do or how to do it, but He does.

I believed that verse, and I believed in Debby. She may not know what she can accomplish, but I believe in her possibility, I believe that she will do what she puts her heart to, and it is not about our accomplishment in helping her, but rather her ability to accomplish her goal in her timing and as she directs.

The buy in, sure I may believe that Debby can do it, but not everyone did. It was clear at the next staff meeting that the line was drawn between the old school of thought of maintenance and protection and the new school of thought of empowerment and possibility. Some of the staff team were overjoyed that we could proceed with a plan of support for Debby and the others were about to lose their cool.

"How can you even think she can do this? She has the intellect of a five year old! You're lining her up for failure!" and "Do you have any idea how dangerous this is?" and "I don't want to have a thing to do with this." My hopes were bruised black and blue, my breath was short, surely my once vibrant complexion was now drained to grey. Fairly closely following that we had one person who quit, one who retired and others who volleyed for their positions.

The ones who were left, I knew could stomach the plan we were about to make. Although, the reluctant ones, I could see had valid points. They were nurturers and protectors, they were excellent caregivers and their motives were to 'care for'. So I put that bit of knowledge into my cap and was careful with my approaches, I tried hard to involve them in the processes.

The others on the team were full of life and creativity. They were the possibility types, full of suggestions, they knew Debby best and saw her potential, and they were absolutely integral in the journey ahead.

Backing up a little, I want to share an experience I had prior to taking the position as Supervisor. It was lunch time and I had decided to eat at a little department store café, if anyone is from my generation, you will know the type I mean. Soup de jour is beef barley or chicken noodle, the best entrée is the hot hamburger sandwich smothered in gravy, salad is coleslaw and pop is always out of the fountain, but most people pick coffee, because it is endless. The waitresses wore polyester in endless shades of mocha and mustard and always wore a little apron. Don't forget the counter, with the line of little stools that swivel and are attached to the ground. All the sandwiches are served on the square sandwich white bread, but to change it up you can get it toasted.

So there I was in this department store cafe, munching on chicken fingers and fries, with a side of coleslaw, with a watered down diet coke fountain drink when I spotted a colourful and bubbly middle aged lady with a high and sweet, yet loud voice, laughing and coaxing the young woman she was with. I say coaxing, because the young woman looked awkward and reluctant. Which I imagine she would be feeling. Most people in their twenties can walk independently, and since this woman was not blind, or hearing impaired, or non-verbal, or immobile, there appeared to be no reason why she would need assistance. To make things even more socially awkward, the lady being led was holding a stuffed animal, a husky dog I think.

Clang, clang, clang, clang!! Let me explain what I mean. While in college, the Dean of our program taught a course called current issues. He taught us that people with disabilities may draw attention in public by things that are unusual and are outside of the normal understanding. This could be particular traits, behaviours, or anything that is visually associated with their disability. I think of this woman, and the only visible sign of her disability was slight palsy on one side of her body causing her to walk with a slight limp and it also slightly affected the mobility of the arm on the same side. That's it. So our professor would call this a clanger. He went on to explain, that sometimes we add to that clanger, by adding clothing that none of us would wear, or hairstyles that none of us would choose, or even in some cases a helmet or other protective or assistive device, which would layer another clanger on the clanger, and soon the person would be making so much non-auditory noise that they were set apart from the normal. This in turn creates fear in people, which can create an environment for people to bully, or respond with ignorance, or in many cases avoid contact, or perhaps make misconceptions about the person. So instead of seeing a person for who they really are, they make a label based on the clangers. I'm sure some may come to your mind.

So there I am, chomping down my chicken strips, losing my mind. Counting the clangers on this young woman, I thought I might choke as they added up. Clanger number one, holding the hand of a staff person amplifies, this person is an eternal child. Clanger number two, stuffy toy, need I say more, how many twenty something people out shopping do you see sporting a stuffy? Clanger number three, buzz cut, was this a male or female person? Clanger number four, the condescending coaxing of the staff person indicated that this young woman was unable to be independent and required a mother figure.

I met Debby a number of months later and felt that the first thing she needed to know was what was normal and appropriate for a young woman of her age, what do other people in their mid-twenties do? I saw so much possibility in her. I wonder if she ever realized that she can love things and ideas and themes that aren't associated with primary and toddler aged children.

Many years ago, Wolf Wolfensberger developed a theory called Social Role Valorization. It included some ideas about negative social roles that people are put into when they have a disability, I'm going to keep it simple, because if you google SRV, you will find paper after paper on in-depth SRV studies and commentaries. The role that defined Debby until this point was 'eternal child'. She never grew up.

Other people, because of their behaviour, or the way they look might be labeled 'deviant'. These are stereotypes or assumed roles that aren't based on fact, but rather perception. They are negative and create a social response that is negative.

In a nutshell, it was our job to try to erase those stereotypes, to find Debby's strengths and unique gifts, things that make her who she is and define her as a valuable, beautiful member of our community. We were to help her believe these things about herself and then have the expectation that we and the community would respond with positive social roles for her. Social roles such as, sister, friend, commuter, artist, employee, horse lover, volunteer, hard worker, kind person and the list goes on and on. These roles any of us could have, disability or not.

Happy hour, the sweet spot between arriving home from the farm where Debby spent her days, and supper time, the glaring contest between roommates across the table. Debby was down in her little den, nestled in her comfy spot. She would curl her feet up under her and flick the T.V. channels endlessly looking for the same familiar cartoons. I knew all was good when I heard the familiar psshtt of the Coca Cola can being cracked open.

Quietly I made my way through the kitchen and slipped into the den. "Hey Deb, gotta minute?"

Raising one eye brow and curling the side of her mouth up in suspicion, she muttered "sure."

"Do you mind if I sit here beside you?"

She smiled much more genuinely, she liked these girl talks and I think we genuinely enjoyed each other's company.

"So I've been thinking about what you said about moving out, and wondering where we should start. And I kind of noticed that lots of the stuff you like and do doesn't always look like someone who might be in their twenties. Do you think we could start talking about that?"

"I guess so."

Now I had her attention, and I truly believe she had no idea what I meant, cartoons, stuffies, kid oriented things had never been something she ever was taught to grow out of. So delicately I tried to tip toe in a non-offensive way.

"Let's go look at your room Deb, would that be okay with you?"

"I guess."

Up the two steps we trod, down the hallway, flicked the light on.

"What do you see?"

Between the two of us we talked about the items we saw, posters of the hulk, Cinderella, my little pony, crayons, colouring books, lots of music tapes, and oodles and oodles of stuffed animals of every kind. This was such a delicate issue, I thought to myself, how do I start?

"Well, I'm thinking if I went to the bedroom of a twenty something year old woman" Yes, woman, Debby wasn't used to being called a woman. "She might have some books, a stereo, like you have, tapes, like you have, she might have a floral wall paper border, if she had pictures, they might be of people she loves, or of flowers or landscapes or animals. I don't think she would have posters on her walls of cartoon characters though, she might have a few stuffed animals, but I don't think I would see her in public with them. What are your thoughts?"

"I guess so." She said

How can one be delicate with the truth, how do you speak the truth with a deep care and concern, with sensitivity toward the one who's hearing it? My heart sank, and I'd hoped I was kind and non-confrontational.

"You know, there's nothing wrong with the choices you've made, your room is made up of stuff you like, but I want to help you understand who you are as an adult, because you've said you want to have your own place, like other people your age, so I really think that begins with you believing that you are an adult, and exploring what that means."

She had a little grin. "Ya, okay."

Debby wasn't a woman of many words, and I was always concerned that she was just agreeing with me, just for the sake of it. I always hoped she would really grasp what this new adult life she wanted entailed.

"I know something I could imagine you would like on your walls Debby."

"Ya?"

"Pictures of horses, maybe a wallpaper border with galloping horses printed on it. I know you love them don't you."

Her face lit up. "Ya, I do."

"So here's the thing" I said, "You think all of this over, and if ever you want to redecorate your room, and exchange the cartoony/stuffy stuff, you know where I am right? Just let me know and we'll go shopping, a new bed in the bag, paint, wallpaper, curtains, whatever you want, I'm sure we can manage it in your budget, if that's what you would like. Sound like a plan?"

"Sure."

Week after week, Debby never came to me about the room, or changing things, but she had decided not to take stuffies out into the community anymore, and all staff seemed to be on board as far as age appropriateness and how to teach and encourage her adultness. Things were progressing and we were beginning to see maturity. Staff were including Debby in her decisions, respecting her choices and we had begun the process of teaching community independence skills.

One thing we realized that in order for Debby not to burn out, or get frustrated we needed to teach her in a way that she understood. What we did understand through an MRI was that the left side of Debby's brain was underdeveloped. After some research we put teaching aids together that appealed to a right brain thinker/learner. So many of the worksheets were pictures, with very simple teaching principles. We addressed everything from community safety, bus safety, safe places, safe people, preparing before going. We did simple budgeting, banking, cooking, and meal preparation. Debby started to pack her own lunches, make healthy food choices, and do her own transactions at the bank.

One of the struggles that staff had had in the past was with respect to hygiene, and there are many people we support who get in power struggles with staff in this area. I truly had no idea how to address this, because it was just one of those areas that was awkward, like the age appropriateness. So one day I just sat and had a casual conversation with Debby. I wanted her to see my own struggles and humanness, and somehow tie the bathing issue into it.

"Man, Debby, this morning was such a struggle getting out of bed."

"Really."

"That's why I love my morning pick me up shower. Wakes me up, gets me going."

"Really?"

"Yah, do you feel like that in the morning?"

"Yah, I hate getting up."

"Have you ever tried the morning shower thing?"

"No."

"Do you want to?"

"Yah sure."

That was simply the end of Debby's 'hygiene' struggle. Sometimes we realize that the more choices and freedoms we present, and the less demands we impose, the more responsive people will be to taking personal responsibility. It doesn't mean that we didn't have to teach how to do things properly, and maybe we can make things easier by providing assistive devices and teaching people how to do something, but we should always be ready with creative ideas. It might be as easy as a pump on a shampoo bottle or shower gel or an electric toothbrush, or some different flavoured toothpaste, or some floss picks. Dignity and respect, not demands and indifference.

Several months had passed and I was in the office processing timesheets and doing any number of the cumbersome activities of supervisors. Happy hour had come and I heard staff greeting Debby. I heard her clattering about emptying her lunch kit, and starting supper prep with staff. It wasn't long before she was standing at the office door with a smirk painted on her face. I loved that mischievous look, I knew she was about to bomb me with something.

"Hey, what's up?"

Quietly, almost whispering, Debby had a secret to tell, "Remember that time we talked? You know in my room?"

"You mean about redecorating?"

"Yah." she smiled as if she just finished a race and won the medal. "I'm ready to do that."

Elation welled up in my heart. I wanted to cartwheel down the hallway. She'd heard, and she'd understood, and she was beginning to feel that adultness! And she remembered! She remembered to come and tell me, she had had time to process and make it her own, on her own time, with her own ideas.

"That's awesome Debby!" I wondered if she saw my heart flip-flopping with joy by the expression on my face. "So any thoughts about colours and what types of pictures?"

"I like horses."

By the end of the month Debby's room was painted a fresh soft grey, the kid stuff was packed away, a new burgundy bed in the bag was purchased with a beautiful matching valance and Debby had chosen a lovely horse border and picked out some framed prints with horses. She was so proud of her choices and took pride in caring for her new place. My heart swelled for her achievement, for her choices, and for her newfound empowerment.

After about a year, Debby was ready to do her first community independence task, with no support from staff. We had spent the last year doing everything with her, shadowing her and fading support, small bits at a time. Finally the day came.

"Okay, Debby, just go over what you're going to do today okay?"

"I do my banking, then walk to the buck store and meet you there."

"That's right, and if you have any problems what will you do?"

"Call you."

"And if you can't get a hold of me?"

"Get help from someone like police or a shop clerk."

"Right, so you ready?"

"Yah."

Away she went. All the necessary stuff in her pack. All the necessary skills taught and proven. My plan was to drive two blocks up and watch her from a distance without her knowing and make sure she was crossing roads safely and taking the right route and getting to the buck store safely.

There I was, covertly waiting for Debby's grand exit from the bank, and there she was off to the races. I watched her cross the first street safely, and away I went to the next block up to wait. And wait I did, and no Debby. How could I have lost sight of her?

It was a frantic 10 minutes of driving, up and down, side to side and finally I relinquished my plan to keep looking and parked outside the buck store. I jumped out of the car and ran to the door.

"Where ya been?" Debby's head popped out of the heavy glass door and peeked around the corner to where I was standing hyperventilating.

"Seriously?? Where were you? I was following you a couple of blocks up and I lost you right away, what happened?"

"I came out of the bank and I needed to use the washroom, so I went to Subway to use theirs. The washroom was out of order there, so I went to the library and used theirs. Then I came here."

No problem, I thought, no problem. Me, the mother hen, clucking around frantically and she was there with all her critical thinking skills, safely getting from the bank to the buck store with no problems. Who was the one with the problem? I was, because I was filled with fear and didn't believe deep down that she could do it. But I have to say, I was thrilled to share the experience with the staff team. We all laughed at the image created of me frantically driving up and down the streets.

We realized that day that Debby was ready to use the community independently. From then on, she would come home from the farm each day and use happy hour to walk up town on her own. Maybe do her banking, buy something at the buck store, go to the library or just go for a walk. And each time she came back safely just in time for supper. Over the next several months she had lost about 25 pounds and blossomed into a beautiful young lady. She was tanned and slim and confident. She was happy and beautiful.

Debby had come to the point where she realized she was ready. We also as an agency believed she was ready. We didn't believe that Debby could live completely on her own, but we did believe that she could do it with support and with the presence of a supportive roommate. After some searching for the right supportive roommate and the right place, after several months of preparing a funding plan for the authorities, the time had finally come. It took Debby a couple of years to accomplish her goal, but accomplish it she did.

There are so many other things that Debby did during that time, critical life decisions and each decision she handled with eloquence and ease. We taught her how to seek advice when it came to health issues, that we were not the experts, but her health nurse was, and so was her Doctor. There were relationship issues she had to learn how to deal with. And each time it took us giving her ideas, educating her and then backing off for her to choose how she would deal with it.

In my office I was digging though some archives and I found a picture of Debby that was taken around five years prior. She was pale, overweight, and I couldn't tell if she was male or female. She had an angry look of frustration on her face, I barely recognized her. I quietly thanked God for how she had blossomed and become victorious in her life. I put the picture in a file and put it away. Several days later I picked up some photos of a backyard birthday barbecue we had had for Debby's roommate. As I was flipping through them I was stunned at a picture of Debby. She was absolutely radiant, her hair was longer and shiny, she was slim and tanned and she had the most exuberant smile that I had ever seen.

Like the butterfly emerging from the confines of her cocoon,

Breaking forth from the tiny room,

That fenced her in, stealing time,

Alas, spring forth, spread wings, and fly.

Chapter 5 – Uncaged

If ever there was a person who I longed to see the well of life burst forth water, it was for James. I found it hard to believe that in this great nation of Canada, one of our citizens could be so devalued, so destitute of people's compassions, treated almost as if an animal being kept alive, until it was no longer. You may think I'm exaggerating, but that was exactly my impression as I entered into his life.

I don't know even how to start to describe James, but I want to paint such a picture that you are taken to a place where you are sitting right beside him.

James was a younger man, he was completely blind, his hearing, however, could be described as acute. James could walk with assistance, but not for any length. He was fed through a G-Tube.

His favourite activity was listening to music, and all day, between 'feeds', James would sit on a mat in front of the stereo and listen to music. Until that is, the cd ended. At which time James would yell to get the attention of the attending staff member, and if the yelling didn't work, James would hit himself in the head until he bled.

Consequently, James had a helmet, so that when he hit himself, he wouldn't do damage, like making his nose bleed, or splitting his skin open, or giving himself a black eye. The softshell helmet was designed in such a way that it covered his forehead, temples and a strip of padded leather came down and protected his nose. These types of items are necessary for people's protection at times. And since I never really witnessed this type of self-injury, I had to keep my questions and opinions to myself, since I was just learning.

I watched James closely for several weeks and observed many things. The helmet never really came off. Consequently, there were dents in the side of his head where the pressure points were. When the music stopped, staff most times didn't respond, so James would yell, and yell, still no response, and after several minutes James would begin to self-injure. The staff documented frequency and duration and type of self-injury. But for some reason, they didn't respond to James' initial request and loud voice, for the music to be changed.

So I thought, maybe I should start to model. I'd learned in college that sometimes it's our actions that will speak louder than words. So each time the first loud voice came out of James, I got up and went to him.

"Do you want another cd on James?"

The yelling stopped.

"Let's see, Great Big Sea? Michael Buble? Sarah MacLaughlin?"

It seemed James didn't care, I didn't see his face change at any of them. But I had noticed before that James liked the driving, thumping of the celtic style. So I put on Great Big Sea and James proceeded to rock on the mat, back and forth and back and forth, and them the real sign of James' happiness came. The raspberries! James would blow raspberries when he was happy. For the time being, that sound was music to my ears!

Even though I would model this response, the staff just didn't seem to agree. So I would talk to them about it, and let them know that I've noticed that the self-injury doesn't occur if we respond more promptly to James' need. The excuses flew, "we have other things to do!" and "Can't you see we are busy with other people too?"

So I started to observe what they were doing when these events occurred, the house was always staffed with two staff to three individuals. And most of the time, when these occurrences took place, the staff were sat at the kitchen table, sometimes chatting, sometimes texting, but I would say they were never run off their feet to the point that they couldn't respond to this minor request to change the cd in the stereo.

"We want you to get a PRN for James! We are tired of his yelling, we can't work and it's really disturbing."

A PRN is a medication that is given only when necessary. In this case, staff were requesting that I speak to the Doctor about getting an Ativan prescription. I kept going back to my college days. I learned that when trying to manage behaviours we should try to use the least restrictive approach first, then work from there if necessary. In James' case, the least restrictive approach would be to listen and respond to that first cue that he needed help. All he really wanted was music, a simple request.

So as a team we met and discussed these less restrictive approaches. Many jumped on board and others continued to press for the PRN. We continued to document and baseline and then I called in a Behaviour Consultant who could witness what was going on and be a third person to write up a response plan. The plan wasn't rocket science. When James begins to show signs of agitation, attend to him. Yes, it was a little more in depth than that.

Little by little, the response time got better, and we began removing the helmet for more extended periods of time. But we also realized that there were so many other things in James life that were disturbing, other times when the self-injury would escalate.

For people like James, the simple things in life should bring pleasure. Like music, sleep time, bath time, maybe a walk, pleasant smells, the things that many of us take for granted. At this point James was really participating in one thing that brought him pleasure. That was sitting on his mat listening to music. It was the only time we witnessed the raspberry blowing.

Mario, a lovely and gentle man, worked day shift on occasion at the home, and each time he did, he would take James to a neighbouring group home, up the hill. It was a beautiful and peaceful place, and they had a lovely big Jacuzzi tub with a lift.

There was no tub at James' house, it was taken out and a shower had been put in its place to allow for the commodes to be rolled in and out. So person gets undressed, sits on the commode, and rolls in the shower, quick rinse with the handheld shower, shampoo, soap, rinse and out. Next! It smacked of the assembly line that Dale spoke about in the institution.

Unfortunately, this approach provided no pleasure to James, he hit his head so violently during this time that he had to wear his helmet in the shower, so he had two helmets, a dry one and a wet one. What was he trying to tell us? Maybe something like this.

"If they would just slow down, this chair feels strange, I'm cold. The water feels like pins and needles stabbing my skin, it hurts, and the soap in my eyes is stinging me. The water just burned me! The smell of the shampoo is making me feel sick. I'm cold."

I was so thankful for Mario, who somehow empathized with James. I knew he felt his pain, and I knew he longed for a change. But how could that happen? James had lived here for twenty some years, gradually digressing to this point. But Mario understood that there was another place where James made raspberries and that was at the other home, in the Jacuzzi tub. So Mario would linger in that place, 'wasting' time, which in my book, was time well wasted.

I really want to celebrate staff who can find those little meaningful things, and who can put self aside and completely, no holds barred, support people in living happy, peaceful and oftentimes exuberant lives.

For Mario, taking James to the other house meant that he had to lift James out of his chair, put him in the front seat of the car. Fold up the wheelchair, which comes apart in many parts, try to find a little place to put it in his little car. Reassemble the chair on the other side, lift James out of the car. Get James ready for the bath, use the mechanical lift to get James in the tub safely. And then do the whole take down and reassembling and lifting on the other side after the bath. But Mario understood the true value of his sacrifice, and in this case it was expressed in raspberries.

Mario was one of those people who carried someone over the threshold to triumph, it may seem simple, but James' simple pleasure of the Jacuzzi tub was one of his triumphs.

While at our 'headquarters' one day, I heard that this house where James went to use the tub, had a vacancy, and for some reason it just felt like the answer! Why couldn't James live there? It was quiet, which James liked, and didn't have where he lived. His current roommates paced, excessively, and because James had such acute hearing, he often found the repetitious noise of the pacing on linoleum to be agitating. His brow would furrow and he would rock back and forth to try and comfort himself.

It had the Jacuzzi tub, which meant that James could use it daily. The staff were calm and supportive and the tone in the house was that of peace. So I went to my supervisor and asked if it could be a possibility.

The most important thing by then was getting the family's buy in. So I contacted James' brother, who didn't have a super close relationship with James, but did make himself present for meetings and for stopping by the house on occasion. He went to view the other house and felt to mention it to a friend of the family who made monthly visits to James. He thought she would be a better gauge of how this might work for James.

"What on earth do you think you're doing? I'm a registered nurse, and I know about these types of things, if you take James out of this home that he's lived in for twenty odd years he will die. I know about these things!"

Thump, bang, thump, bang, I could feel my heart banging against my chest, my breath was getting more and more shallow and I was shaking like a leaf. I hate confrontation, but I believe so strongly in advocating for people that don't have a voice.

I tried so delicately to explain some of the observations that I had made about James' environment and I tried to describe how happy he was with the Jacuzzi tub and how we observed no self-injury there, only contentment and happiness when he was in the house. I tried to explain to her that if we just tried it, and if he didn't adjust we could always bring him back. But she just wouldn't have it. I invited her to see the home, but again her heels were dug in.

"I've known this family for years and when his Mother died I made a promise that I would watch out for him. I believe I'm making the right call, James will die if he makes such a drastic change. I'm not even willing that he should try it." She was clearly adamant about her decision.

"Maybe could you think about it? Just call me when you've had time to consider the reason we feel it would be better."

"I don't know what you people think, and I don't know what your motive is, whether it's more cost effective, or what your long term objectives are, but forget it. James will stay where he is, I promised his mother."

Oh that sinking feeling. Defeat crept over me like a densely endless fog. I was hurt because of the insinuations regarding our motive, I was more hurt for James though. We would now have to make do, I saw no way here to improve, just maintain, which had been done for so many years. Then the anger came flooding in. "Oh yah" I thought to myself, "We all have to go to someone else's house to enjoy a bath! That's normal and right and healthy alright!"

I think I fumed for days, I felt lost and I wanted to climb a mountain and scream. But it wasn't long before my position was to change. Before I came to manage James' home I was told that I would have a position in a day program, which was much closer to home. So I conceded and moved on. Never had I walked away in such defeat and hopelessness. I realized that there wasn't a whole lot else I could do.

James continued, with a few small improvements, and we never had to put the Ativan in place. That was a good thing, and we managed to change his goals so that he could use the Jacuzzi tub at the other house three times a week. We were given a wheelchair van, so that people didn't have to lift James anymore. That was about all we could do to improve James' quality of life.

I went on with my new position, and after about three months I received a phone call from our Quality Assurance Officer.

"Delia, I want to invite you to James' annual plan. It will be held at his new home, the one with the Jacuzzi tub, on Wednesday at 2."

I don't know what changed and what changed the mind of the advocate but it happened. It turns out that James was happy there, he blew raspberries the entire time during the meeting. Triumph.

> Joy arises in the peaceful place,
>
> A symphony of raspberries, the ones you don't taste.
>
> But listening to them fills one's ears,
>
> Trickles down to the heart, then back up in tears.

Chapter 6 – Words Unspoken

Some people are scarier than others. Naomi had that sort of sideways glare and when you received it, the time stood still, and you could see something was brewing, tick tock, tick tock, tick tock, like a bomb ready to blow. Sometimes you're quick enough to use all the non-violent crisis intervention techniques to avoid being the target of her outbursts and sometimes, unfortunately, not.

We were all happily returning from a beautiful time of respite at a retreat centre on the shore of the sea, with lapping waves gently washing the sandy beach and bald eagles soaring in the distance. A sense of enduring joy washed over all of us and lingered on the journey back. Upon arriving back, the joy continued in the unpacking, or so I thought.

Boxes of left over foods, suitcases, and bags of dirty laundry littered the kitchen and living room floors. But we were a crew, a team of worker bees, busy about our business, each to his own.

Naomi was hanging around the kitchen, pitching in, putting this and that away. I was with her, singing the praise of the trip, and what a wonderful time was had, in my high pitched excitement I didn't notice that tell-tale sideways glance. And quick as ever, I realized, far too late, that I was backed into the corner of the kitchen counters. Quick as wildfire in a brittle dry field, she had me in a headlock. It's not like I was scared or anything, just embarrassed that I had found myself in a position that I forever coached staff not to be in.

"Don't find yourself backed into a corner, always have a way of escape." Non-Violent Crisis Prevention 101.

It is times like these that we realize that all is not well. The environment and circumstance around seemed to be appealing, or at least we interpreted things that way. But something was wrong. What was wrong in Naomi's life that led her to lash out like this?

Naomi lived in a nice house, enjoyed activities both at home and in the community, eats good food, has positive family involvement, and is cared for well by her support workers. What could be wrong?

The digging began. We started to ask questions. Are you upset? How do you feel? Why did you get angry? And it seemed with each question we got a yes or no answer, or something monosyllabic with not a whole lot of emotional response behind it. After a while, it occurred to me that Naomi might have a communication disorder, even though she could verbalize with us, it didn't mean that she could really process what we were saying and give an appropriate response. It also didn't mean that she could process her *feelings* into words.

While we may think she is having fun with us and sharing our joy, as in the incident upon returning from the retreat, she could be feeling any number of emotions that she can't process into words or even into expression for that matter. Her countenance presents as flat and expressionless. What if she was tired? What if my high pitched elation was driving her over the edge? What if...? And now what?

After some consultation with parents, staff and our director, we decided to call in a communication consultant. I tell you, the professionals we consult are worth their weight in gold.

Penny was definitely worth her weight in gold, a soft-spoken Scottish woman, I could have listened to her accent for days and not tire of it. She opened her little black bag of tricks and voila! There was the answer! A picture book of emotions! Happy, sad, mad and a hundred other expressions in pictures! Hope was rising! But not only faces to express, but also potential problems in pictures! Too loud, too crowded, too hot, too cold, you name it, if you could experience it, it was there in pictures.

Now, I'm sure to some this might seem super simple, but I'm convinced there are many people out there that are labelled 'behavioural' and desperately need someone to troubleshoot the reasons why. I've seen examples of it everywhere I've been, no exceptions. In fact, there isn't anywhere in three provinces where I've worked that I haven't seen examples of this. There is always a reason why, and it usually lies in a person's inability to communicate their desires, feelings and hopes. As a community it is our human responsibility to advocate, figure it out, celebrate the possibilities and overlook the disability, until, that is, the diagnosis is needed to plan for a positive outcome.

Naomi coveted her little book of treasures and over time she learned that she could let us know ahead of time when something was bothering her. The incidents of violence and aggression drastically decreased. No more cartons of eggs smashed on the floor, cups of tea tossed across the table, or people getting hurt. When she had had enough of an activity, she would point to the appropriate picture and off she went. No struggles, no doubt, just an empowered woman.

Furthermore, Naomi began to plan her own day with a picture calendar that was mounted to the wall with Velcro strips that had times of the day attached to them. Staff would help Naomi pick symbols of activities that she would put on her calendar daily. If for whatever reason she didn't want to do something, she knew she had the power to change it. No longer did she view staff as controlling and unapproachable, now she was a part of her life, empowered to self-direct, empowered to communicate.

Behaviours can be tricky, but it's been my experience that they can always be averted, we can listen, respond and help people develop a personal strategy to express themselves and be empowered to self-direct. There is nothing more rewarding than helping people self- discover, and I believe that all people regardless of the disability can discover, uncover, and recover.

Silent, silent, silent but with words.

Disconnect, somehow, angry and unsure.

Connection, responsive, aliveness on alert.

A new life, a huge smile, from a wonderful new word.

Chapter 7 – Back to the Past

This story has to be one of the most moving stories I've been blessed to be a part of. I've never seen a person emerge from the proverbial pit like Bob did. It's not like I didn't go into Bob's living situation as Team Leader without a certain amount of fear and trepidation. My orientation was short, and the information was scant.

I was informed that "We aren't really sure what's up with Bob, he just hurts himself all the time. But he's seeing a Psychiatrist, and mental health isn't really sure what's wrong. There is medication, so we are trying to get the self-injury under control. When he hurts himself, we just document it."

That's it? I couldn't believe my ears. Being an action person, I didn't know what to do with that information. How do you just follow someone and ask him to go to his room when he begins to punch the living daylights out of himself?

How do you count those punches, one, two, three, four, fifteen, sixteen. Oh, and time the duration and try to offer some pillows and balls as he throws himself violently on the bed, thrashing out of control. I'd seen self-injury, but this took the cake. Frankly, I was completely freaked out and so were his support workers, none of which had any post-secondary training in the field of developmental services or behaviour analysis. Which, sadly, was the reality of isolated rural communities.

How do you begin taking care of this? Reports said that Bob was non-verbal, and staff reported that he would just mimic you if you asked him questions, repeating the last thing you said. He hardly ever got out, even to get his hair cut, he had to go to a person who was a long-time family friend, who had no experience or certificate to cut hair. Apparently the hairdresser in town wouldn't see him anymore because he had an 'outburst' last time he went to see her.

There lay Bob, day after day on his bed, then he would be begin pacing like a hungry lion an hour before meal times, and staff would try desperately to manage while making dinner. Bob was black and blue up and down from temple to knee from the violent hits that he inflicted upon himself. I desperately needed to find the solution.

Over time we managed to pull the base line information together and realized that there were certain times where the behaviours became more severe. Think about it, for Bob, what would be the only times that he would be stimulated or sensory overloaded? Sure enough, we realized that meal times were filled with smells, sounds of preparation, the heat of food cooking and the promise of delicious tastes and diverse textures. The base-line revealed an escalation of anxiety almost to the minute, one hour prior to meal times.

Strategies were developed to deal with that anxiety, which included Bob helping with supper preparation, purposefully letting Bob know how long supper would be. Offering other sensory activities during the supper preparation hour. These included listening to a favourite movie or radio station, having a massaging foot bath, or playing harmonica for roommates. We realized over time that we wanted this to be star time for Bob and over time we noticed that the redirection had shifted focus for Bob, but also brought meaningful, valuable other activities into his life that weren't necessarily there before.

It is always delightful to glean insight from family members. Somehow as service providers we can be so compartmentalized. We are the professionals, we know what's best. But do we? In Bob's case, Mom was vital in filling in the blanks. Trips to Mom's house were prime opportunities to watch Bob use the environment he had grown up in. At his childhood home Bob navigated the whole house independently, he also fixed his own coffee and carried it to his favourite place in the home to drink it. He followed through on Mom's suggestions of helping with tasks that we wouldn't have believed he could do, like wrapping gifts and picking vegetables from the garden.

After transferring this understanding into Bob's current home environment, we set up the coffee pot in a place where he could easily access it. Bob was delighted, a simple step of empowerment and the autonomy to use his own environment all of a sudden created a sense of value, he stood up straighter, he began to engage with those around him, and low and behold, he spoke.

Bob began to respond to our questions with more than a head shake or nod. Emotion started to fill his face, emotion other than that of frustration and anger that is. And we absolutely loved engaging with Bob. He began to respond to choices based on his own needs and desires, not what he thought the staff members wanted him to say.

The first time I saw this happen, Bob was heading out to a neighbouring community. We had learned to help Bob pack a backpack of sensory items to help him cope when he was feeling anxious in the community. Also a drink and a snack. Because we were in a rush, I packed the pack for him on one occasion. I let him know his back pack was ready near the door. I suggested he check to make sure that everything that he wanted to take was in it. I had to chuckle when I saw Bob take absolutely everything out of his backpack and repack it with entirely different items than I had chosen.

Out went the orange fluffy duster, and the purple sensor ball, tentacles tickling and wiggling. Gone was the red cushion for squeezing replaced with the blue striped one. In goes the big white fluffy duster and the big green ball with the short rigid tentacles. Oh well, what do they say? Out with the old, in with the new.

I've learned not to make assumptions about what people want, even the minor things. Things that seem insignificant to me might be colossal to a person who hasn't had a whole lot of autonomy and decision making in their lives.

I wonder if Bob repacked the backpack just because he could. Was it that he really wanted the replaced items? After all, I was pretty sure that I knew what his favourite things were, or did Bob repack it just to practice his own decision making and realize his autonomy? Truly, I will never know, but I smile and I'm humbled when I see people living in freedom and trusting that their choices and uniqueness will be valued and respected by those around them.

Not only did Bob's home life blossom, but even members of the community were noticing, Bob went almost daily to have a beverage at the local coffee shop, he enjoyed haircuts at the hairdresser who had originally been afraid of him, he did his banking, went for lunches at local restaurants, went to the farmer's market, went to visit family and friends and all of sudden there were no more outbursts, Bob had learned to communicate when he'd had enough of any given activity, and we had learned to listen and respect him. Several people remarked on the transformation, marvelling at the difference.

Bob also began to talk, he was no longer non-verbal, because people were listening, he began to ask for things, answer questions and chain words to sentences.

This transformation was worth celebrating, with harmonicas we celebrated, we danced in the kitchen, we decorated the walls, even though Bob couldn't see it, we described the colours, he smelled the balloons, and out came the tongue to explore what that smell tasted like. We rejoiced in his smile, like sunshine it warmed the hearts of all it fell upon.

There was such a change in Bob that even his Mom commented how he was just like he was when he was seventeen before he went blind. He had gone back to the past and rediscovered his identity. Every life is beautiful, some are ripe for discovery others begging rediscovery.

>Buried somewhere deep within,
>
>Is one who wants to lift his chin,
>
>To revisit the days long gone by,
>
>When he was loved and filled with life.

Chapter 8 – A Team Triumphant

As a team we realized that we had a lot of work to do when it came to educating the community with regards to how people with disabilities should be treated. They have rights and they should be treated with the same dignity and respect as anyone else in community. But in fairness, we don't really understand the full scope of their adversity. The community doesn't understand it either.

As Mary experienced with the police, the one young constable thought that people with disabilities are "punished this way". I experienced a similar incident when I accompanied a lady to a Doctor's appointment. After the Doctor examined her for a hernia, he proceeded to demean her as she was lying on the examining table with her shirt up, by slapping her belly several times and saying "You know what your problem is don't you? You are a big fatty!" This poor woman smiled and nodded her head, thinking that he was right. I knew I couldn't get in a confrontation with him, after all he was the one specialist in the area, best to leave sleeping dogs lie. However, when I left the appointment with her we had a discussion about his inappropriateness and that he shouldn't have treated her like that. She shrugged it off, as if it was another offense in a long list of them.

As an agency we continued to discuss the inappropriateness of community members and their attitudes, but we were sure that it wouldn't be us that would change attitudes. It had to come out of the passion of the people who were living subject to such negative biases.

The conversations began and a new group was formed. A group of self-advocates, persons with disabilities, who would share their stories with whomever would listen. A couple of them enrolled in the public speaking course at the local college, we helped them write and practice communicating what they wanted to be treated like. That they were people of possibility first, not of disability. They wanted to communicate that they are eager to contribute to their communities, they want to be treated equally, have opportunity, and have the same respect by community medical and emergency personnel as would people who don't have disabilities.

This group was self-led, we supported them when they needed us to, but they made their own decisions, and set and achieved their own goals. Soon they were educating students at the college, doing presentations for rotary and various other community members. We watched them triumph and change attitudes as well as gain more respect and exposure in the community.

We loved celebrating with them, one gentleman loved to tell his story of how he has gone from teenagers spitting in his pizza to having his story heard and his opinions valued. He was so proud that he wasn't satisfied and wanted to do more. The group decided that they wanted to be seen as respected workers in the community.

We helped them contact the media studies program at the local community college and after some letters and meetings a few volunteer students said they would help the group do a video highlighting the successes of people with disabilities working and volunteering. These young college students really had no idea how their lives would be impacted over the course of the next few months.

The bell on the front door jangled and eyes darted toward the entrance. Flushed face and tentative, a young man in his early twenties with hands dug deep in pockets lankily strode into the day program facility. His nervousness was more apparent than he probably cared to admit. "I'm here about the video?" It wasn't long before he was welcomed by more than a handful of participants who were eager and excited to get to work.

The group loved Dan, he had a quiet gentle demeanor and listened assertively. He had great leadership skills, was a servant leader, and was willing to go above and beyond the call of duty for the cause. After a few months he had helped the group to develop a script that communicated how employment and volunteerism not only helped develop people with disabilities, but more importantly, contributed to local businesses and celebrated community in its truest sense.

Before long the lights, camera and action were well on the way and various people were being interviewed including employed people, their employers, family members and community members. They told of how employment and volunteerism contributed to their self-esteem and gave them more confidence. Employers testified to the fact that their employees with disabilities were dedicated, hardly ever late or absent and enthusiastically finished tasks with diligence. Most show a longevity and loyalty to their companies that isn't commonly seen these days.

After about six months, the group had a finished product that was a beautiful sight to see. Dan and his team had produced something profoundly professional, a work of art crafted by a group of first year media studies students. The group beamed and began to plan to unveil the video.

The big day came, and many dignitaries, family members, community members and employers were at the unveiling. The group's delegate spoke of their pride in the project as well as the deep respect and connection they had with Dan and his team. I loved how Dan responded.

With tears in his eyes, this young man Dan came forward with a newfound confidence. He told the audience how his life had changed in the past few months. He said he had no idea that people with disabilities could do so much and that never again would he view people through a foggy lens again. Visibly touched and inspired Dan teaches us that we need to see people with eyes wide open, unfettered by preconceived ideas, broken free from fear and unbelief.

This video was such a macro accomplishment, the team's public speakers showed it for years to come to various community groups like Rotary, Chamber of Commerce, colleges and government officials, who knew that this team would be integral in inspiring people in all walks of life. A team triumphant, a community benefitted, the world a better place, one person, one team at a time.

Intricate mosaic of beautiful colours and textures,

Lovingly intertwined into rich fabric.

This is community at its richest,

This is community at its best.

Epilogue

Is there anything richer than life experiences that mould and artistically and meticulously recreate our character? The past fifteen years working with people with disabilities has done just that, made me who I am today.

Sometimes I believe God uses the most unlikely routes to maturity and character reformation. I'm one hundred percent convinced that I'm a different person today than what I was that first day in college. The most unlikely, often challenging situations have formed me. There is a saying, "The stronger the wind blows, the deeper the roots grow." I can attest to this, many times I could have taken the easy route, I could have turned a blind eye, walked away from the tough stuff, but where would I be today? Not much further ahead.

I look around me today, I look around for impossible situations, and choose to stand and laugh in the face of fear.

When it comes to my views of those who are living with barriers, often through no fault of their own, I believe that for everyone, triumph is on the doorstep, just waiting, patiently for someone to reach out for the handle, turn it and push it open.

We all have these opportunities in life, you may be thinking of someone right now who could be encouraged, believed in, or in some cases rescued. Empowerment is only a step away. Words are powerful, we can speak life, belief and possibility into those in our world.

I'm so thankful for those who have shown me in my life that I can live courageously, not just in my life but I can live courageously for others and encourage them to do so too.

Life is birthed in belief. I'm thankful that God showed me how precious life is, that He showed me that all life is worthwhile, fearfully and wonderfully made. Perhaps how we treat others, especially those who are devalued is a test of our character. Who knows? How many people are we passing the test with in our lives? What awesome possibility there is to show character, maybe even on our own doorsteps!

I hope these beautiful stories have been an encouragement to you, thank you so much for celebrating with me as I've shared these stories that have begged to be told. May I have the blessing and may you too have the blessing of finding "Triumph on Doorstep".

Thomas
250-385-3422
225.